Statue of Liberty

Laura Marsh

New York

For all who seek liberty: may it be realized and sustained —L.F.M.

A National Geographic Kids Book
Published by Random House Children's Books under license.
A division of Penguin Random House LLC
1745 Broadway, New York, NY 10019
penguinrandomhouse.com
rhcbooks.com

Designed by Lauren Sciortino

The publisher would like to thank Matt Housch, historian, Statue of Liberty National Monument (National Park Service); Mariam Jean Dreher, literacy reviewer; and Michelle Harris, fact-checker.

Library of Congress Cataloging-in-Publication Data is available upon request.
ISBN 978-1-4263-7828-7 (trade paperback) —
ISBN 978-1-4263-7829-4 (lib. bdg)

Manufactured in the United States of America
10 9 8 7 6 5 4 3 2 1

The authorized representative in the EU for product safety and compliance is Penguin Random House Ireland, Morrison Chambers, 32 Nassau Street, Dublin D02 YH68, Ireland, https://eu-contact.penguin.ie.

Random House Children's Books supports the First Amendment and celebrates the right to read.

Publisher's Note

The first inhabitants of the island where the Statue of Liberty now stands were Native American Indigenous peoples. They are known to have lived there since before 1000 C.E. But by the 1600s, European settlers had driven the Native Americans out, with disease, war, and occupation.

Photo Credits

AD: Adobe Stock; AS: Alamy Stock Photo; BI: Bridgeman Images; CD: Corbis Documentary; GC: The Granger Collection; GI: Getty Images; LOC: Library of Congress; MET: Metropolitan Museum of Art; M&IW: The Miriam and Ira D. Wallach Division of Art, Prints and Photographs; MNY: Museum of the City of New York; NYPL: The New York Public Library; SCI: Science History Images

Cover: eneize/AS; (BKGRD), TTstudio/AD; 1, Matej Kastelic/AS; 3, Valentin Wolf/imageBROKER/AD; 4–5, John A. Anderson/AD; 6, PWB Images/AS; 7 (UP), SCI/AS; 7 (LO), Gift of Samuel P. Avery, 1893/MET; 8, International Numismatic Club; 9, Harry G. Sperling Fund, 2014/MET; 10–11, The Picture Art Collection/AS; 12, John Bacaring; 13 (UP), Mirko/AD; 13 (CTR), John Bacaring; 13 (LO), Richard Hamilton Smith/CD/GI; 14, M&IW/Photography Collection/NYPL; 15 (UP), M&IW/Photography Collection/NYPL; 15 (LO), Hemis/AS; 16 (LE), Markus Mainka/AD; 16 (RT), HABS/HAER/HALS/National Park Service/LOC; 17, M&IW/Photography Collection/NYPL; 18 (UP), Historic American Engineering Record/LOC; 18 (LO), Dan Martland; 19 (UP), Alberto-G-R/AS; 19 (CTR), Felix Mizioznikov/AD; 19 (LO), Jay Vizcarra; 20, LOC; 21 (UP), LOC; 21 (LO LE), Amoret Tanner/AS; 21 (LO RT), Sherab/AS; 22 (UP), HUM Images/Universal Images Group via GI; 22 (LO), GC; 23, Avant-Demain/BI; 24, North Wind Picture Archives/AS; 25 (UP), American Institute of Architects/American Architectural Foundation/LOC; 25 (LO), Art Collection 3/AS; 26, GC; 27, American Institute of Architects/American Architectural Foundation/LOC; 28, GC; 29 (LE), MNY; 29 (UP RT), GC; 29 (LO RT), MNY; 30–31, MPI/GI; 31, BI; 32, Apic/GI; 33 (LE), Marian S. Carson Collection/LOC; 33 (RT), M&IW/Photography Collection/NYPL; 35, John Bacaring; 36 (UP), Gwells/Shutterstock; 36 (UP RT), Colin Underhill/AS; 36 (LO LE), Gustavo Enrique Cortez/AS; 36 (LO RT), jordiphotography/AS; 36–37, agrus/AD; 37 (UP), Olha Prokopchuk/AS; 37 (LO RT), maximimages/AS; 37 (LO LE), Mark Waugh/AS; 38, Tada Images/Shutterstock; 39 (LE), Horace Abrahams/Fox Photos/GI; 39 (RT), Bernard Gotfryd/GI; 40, Terese Loeb Kreuzer/AS; 40–41 (BKGRD), chuck/AD; 41, Tada Images/Shutterstock; 42, Jay Vizcarra; 42–43 (BKGRD), chuck/AD; 43, Jay Vizcarra; 44 (UP), M&IW/Photography Collection/NYPL; 44 (LO), John Bacaring; 45 (UP), Wollwerth Imagery/AD; 45 (CTR), kmiragaya/AD; 45 (LO), GC; 46 (UP LE), Paulo/AD; 46 (UP RT), Prismatic Pictures/BI; 46 (CTR LE), SCI/AS; 46 (CTR RT), 24K-Production/AD; 46 (LO LE), Tarker/BI; 46 (LO RT), Collection of the Smithsonian National Museum of African American History and Culture, Gift from the Liljenquist Family; 47 (UP LE), Brian Jackson/AS; 47 (UP RT), M&IW/Photography Collection/NYPL; 47 (CTR LE), Lightfield Studios/AD; 47 (CTR RT), John Bacaring; 47 (LO LE), Richard Hamilton Smith/CD/GI; 47 (LO RT), Bettmann Archive/GI; (VOCAB), Top Vector Studio/AD

Table of Contents

A National Treasure

A huge sculpture towers over boats in New York Harbor. She stands alone and holds a torch high for all to see.

She is the Statue of Liberty.

Around the world, she stands for the United States. She is also a symbol of freedom and democracy.

Since 1886, the Statue of Liberty has stood in her New York home. But it took many years to get her there. Along the way, thousands of ordinary people helped make it happen.

Words to Know

SYMBOL: An object or thing that stands for something else, such as another idea

FREEDOM: The right to think, speak, or act as you want

DEMOCRACY: A system of government where the people have a say in the country's laws and policies

A Great Gift

After the American Civil War, a French historian and a French sculptor worked together on a statue to celebrate the United States. The historian was Édouard de Laboulaye, and the sculptor was Frédéric-Auguste Bartholdi.

Édouard de Laboulaye

Laboulaye and Bartholdi announced that the French people would give a large statue to the American people. They had several reasons for creating the statue. They wanted to celebrate the end of enslavement in the United States. They also wished to mark a hundred years of American independence from British rule.

Lastly, they wished to honor the friendship between France and the United States. For these reasons, the gift was meant to celebrate freedom and friendship.

Frédéric-Auguste Bartholdi

a medal that honors the gift from France to the United States

Words to Know

ENSLAVEMENT: The act of making someone a slave

INDEPENDENCE: The state of not being controlled by others

Designing the Statue

Bartholdi planned for the statue to look like the Roman goddess Libertas, or Liberty. Liberty means that you can make your own decisions and are not controlled by others. The Roman goddess would represent the idea of freedom in the United States.

Roman goddess Libertas on an ancient Roman coin

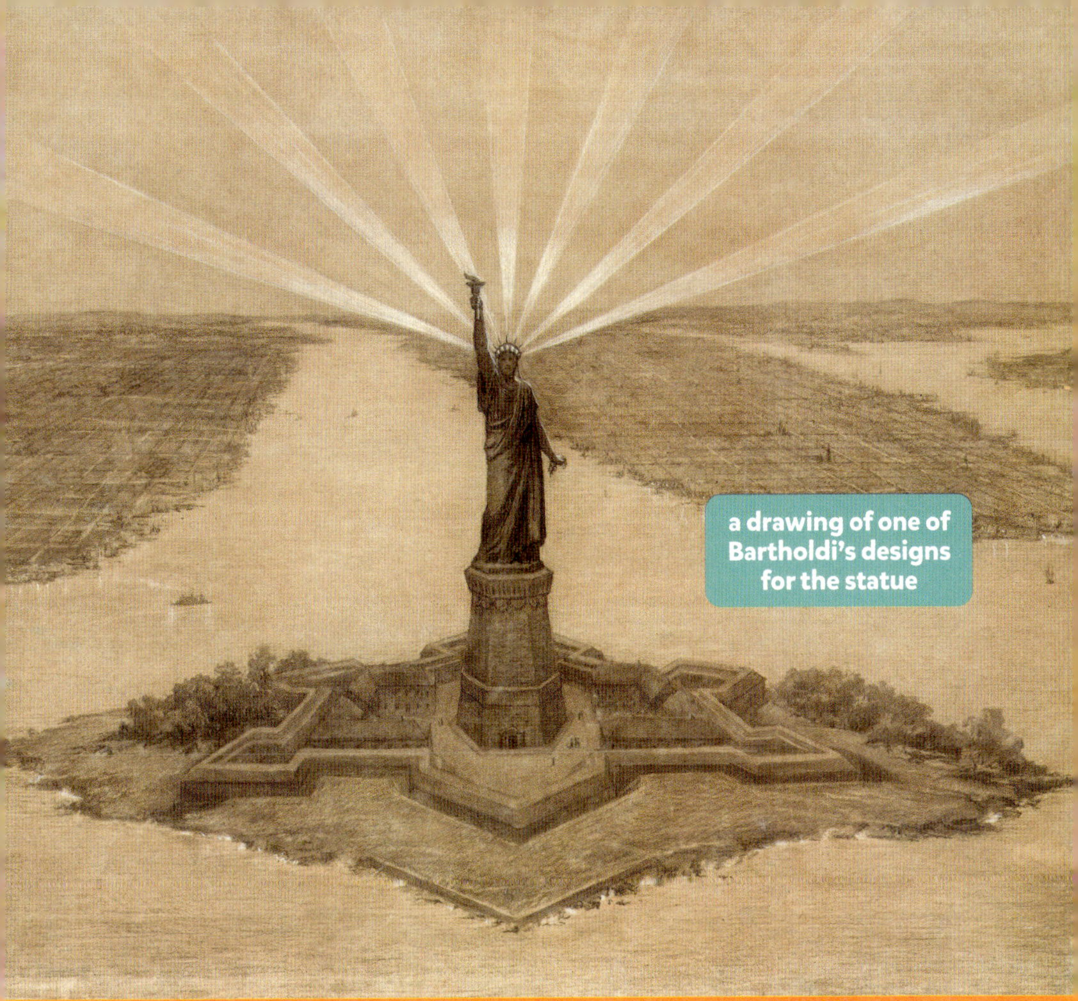

a drawing of one of Bartholdi's designs for the statue

Bartholdi's design showed Liberty dressed in Roman robes and holding a torch. Laboulaye approved the design. They called the statue "Liberty Enlightening the World."

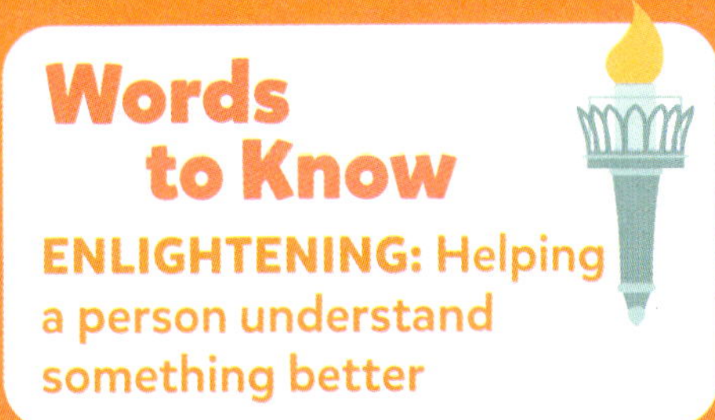

Artwork from 1883 shows New York City and its harbor.

The French would create the statue. The Americans would build the pedestal for it to stand on.

But where would this statue stand? On a trip to the United States, Bartholdi arrived by boat in New York Harbor. There he spotted a tiny island—Bedloe's Island.

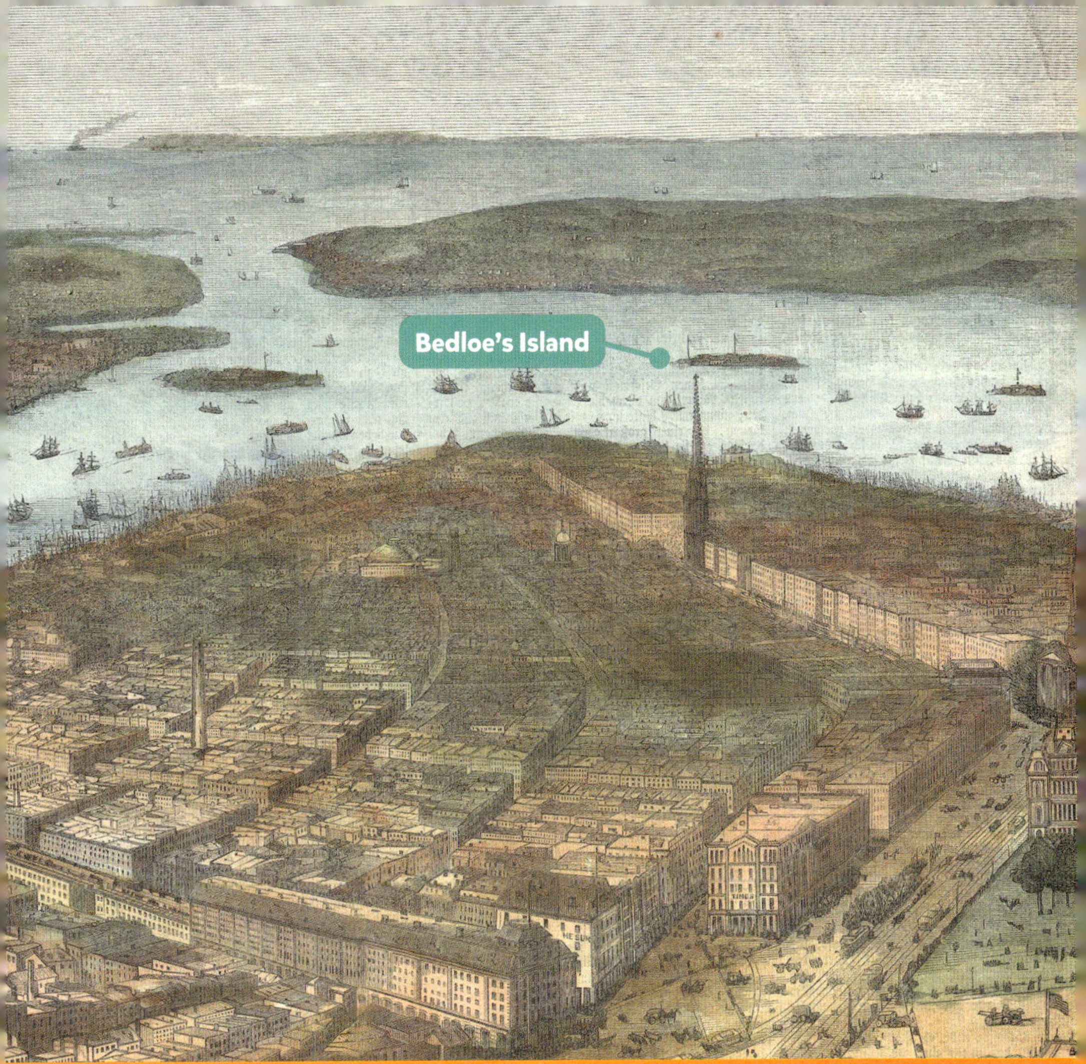

Bedloe's Island

It was the perfect place for his statue. Since the busy harbor was so big, many passengers on ships from all over the world would see the statue.

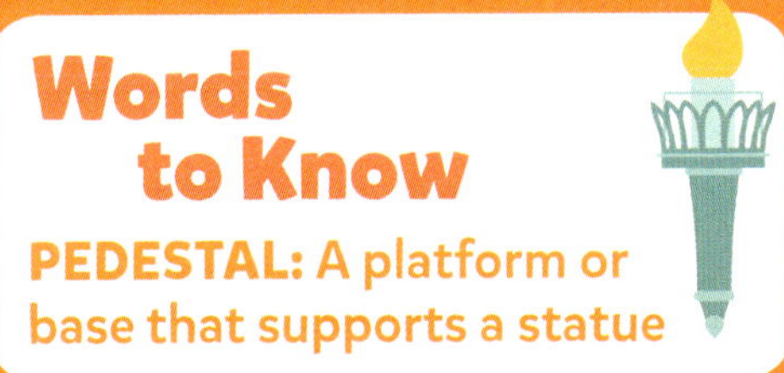

Hidden Meanings

Several parts of the Statue of Liberty are symbols. They have more than one meaning, and they represent bigger ideas.

STONE TABLET: In her left hand, Liberty holds a tablet with the date July 4, 1776, written in Roman numerals. This is the date the Declaration of Independence was adopted. The tablet symbolizes a book of law. It represents the idea that laws in the United States protect people and their freedoms.

Words to Know

DECLARATION OF INDEPENDENCE: A document stating that the American colonies were free from British control

REPRESENT: To stand for something else

That's a FACT!

The tablet is as high as two NBA basketball hoops stacked on top of each other. Its width could fit two cars parked side by side.

CROWN: The spikes on top of Liberty's head look like sunbeams. They form a crown, fitting for a Roman goddess. The crown shows how important the idea of liberty is.

TORCH: The torch's flame is covered with gold. It represents the idea that the light of freedom is being sent out into the world.

BROKEN SHACKLE AND CHAIN: These are at Liberty's feet. They represent the freedom of all people from enslavement and unfair treatment. In earlier designs, Bartholdi's model of Liberty held the broken shackle and chain in her left hand instead of the tablet.

The Monumental Structure

In 1876, Bartholdi and more than 60 workers began building the statue in a metal workshop in Paris. Liberty would be about 151 feet (46 m) tall from her feet to the top of the torch. That's taller than a 10-story building!

Workers built a wooden framework and then put plaster over it. This photo shows the statue's left wrist and hand.

Workers shaped the copper sheets by hammering them. They used new molds created from the plaster model.

The Statue of Liberty, also called Lady Liberty, is made of thin copper sheets. More than 300 copper sheets were hammered and shaped around molds. Then they were attached to each other.

A Green Lady

The copper statue was originally a shiny brown color, like a new penny. But wind, rain, and air slowly changed the color to green. The statue's color took about 30 years to change completely.

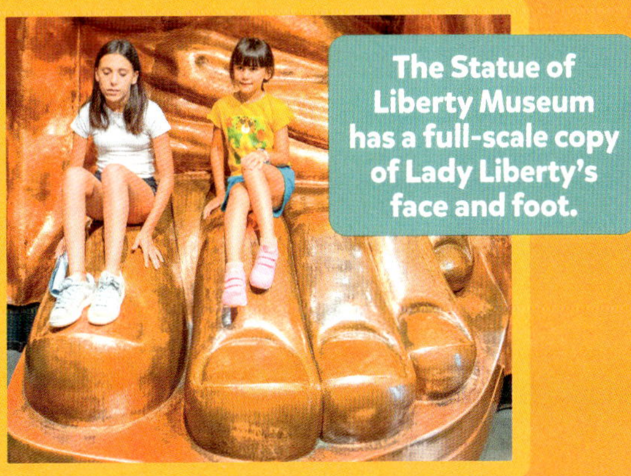

The Statue of Liberty Museum has a full-scale copy of Lady Liberty's face and foot.

The statue needed something built inside of it to hold up the weight of all the copper sheets. So workers built a metal framework to use as a support structure, like a skeleton.

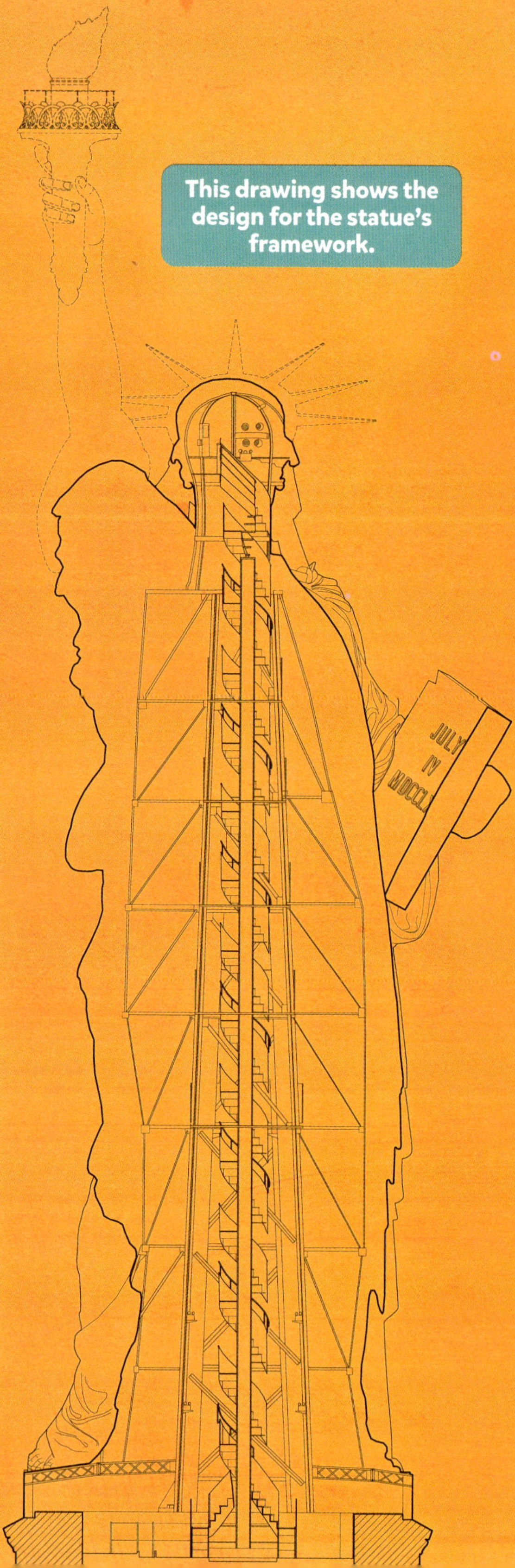

This drawing shows the design for the statue's framework.

That's a FACT!

The company that designed the Eiffel Tower in Paris, France, also designed the skeleton, or support system, for the Statue of Liberty.

In New York Harbor, the statue would need to stand up to high winds and bad weather. The metal framework would allow the statue to move slightly in the wind but not break.

This photo shows the framework for the statue being built in Paris. The statue's head is in the bottom left.

7 Fantastic Facts and Figures

1

Visitors to the statue can climb **162 steps** from the top of the **pedestal to the crown.**

2

The Statue of Liberty sometimes gets **struck by lightning!** But it doesn't cause damage to the statue.

3

The statue's total height is about **305 feet** (93 m) from the pedestal's **foundation to the top of the torch**—that's almost the length of a **football field!**

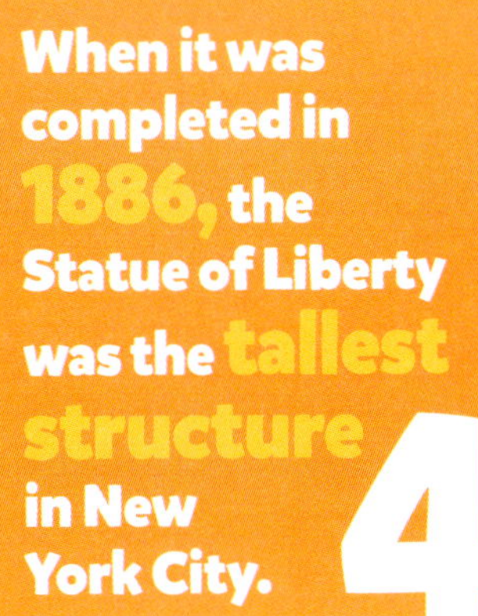

When it was completed in **1886,** the Statue of Liberty was the **tallest structure** in New York City. **4**

Bartholdi kept a **full-size model** of Liberty's **left ear** in his home. It is now in the Bartholdi Museum in Colmar, France. **5**

The **island** on which the Statue of Liberty stands was **renamed Liberty Island in 1956.** Before that it was called Oyster Island, Love Island, and Bedloe's Island. **6**

7 The statue **moves** about **three inches** (7.6 cm) from side to side in **strong winds.**

Building the Statue

Building such a large statue was expensive and took time. In France, a committee held events and sold souvenirs to raise money. They also sold tickets for people to see the statue while it was being built.

In 1878, the statue's head was exhibited in Paris to raise money.

The torch and part of the statue's arm were finished first and put on display in France. People could pay a fee to climb to the top.

Parts of the statue also went to the United States to raise funds. This photo shows the arm and torch displayed in Philadelphia in 1876.

It took about five years to raise the money to build the statue. More than 100,000 French citizens donated.

That's a FACT!

Since its beginning, the image of the Statue of Liberty has been used to sell all kinds of products, such as snacks, lemons, sewing machines, soap, and even umbrellas!

Workers hammer sheets of copper for the statue.

When the statue became too big to fit inside the workshop, construction was moved outside. Eventually, Liberty towered over the rooftops of Paris.

Mom as Model?
Many people have wondered who the Statue of Liberty is modeled after. Some say she looks a lot like Bartholdi's mother. The truth is still a mystery.

After about eight years, the statue was finally completed. It was taken apart and packed into more than 200 crates. Each piece of the statue was carefully numbered so that it could be put back together in New York. The crates were moved by train and then loaded onto a ship.

the Statue of Liberty under construction in Paris in 1884

A Pedestal for Lady Liberty

In 1885, the statue arrived in New York. But the pedestal in the United States was not ready. Construction had stopped because the money had run out.

This artwork shows crowds welcoming the ship carrying Lady Liberty into New York Harbor on June 17, 1885.

one of the pedestal designs that Hunt did not choose

Architect Richard Morris Hunt designed the pedestal. After thinking about many ideas, Hunt decided on an 87-foot (26.5-m) structure made of concrete and granite.

But there would be no Statue of Liberty without a pedestal. Time was running out. Something had to be done.

That's a FACT!

Richard Morris Hunt designed many buildings in the United States, including the front of the Metropolitan Museum of Art in New York City.

Steel beams inside the pedestal would connect to the statue's framework to keep it in place.

Joseph Pulitzer, publisher of *The World* newspaper, had a great idea. He promised to print the name of every person who donated money for the pedestal. No amount was too small.

People all over the country began sending money to the pedestal fund. Schoolchildren collected pennies. Families gave what they could.

In just five months, the rest of the money was raised! Most donations were about a dollar or less. Pulitzer helped Americans feel pride in the statue. They were ready for Lady Liberty to be placed in New York Harbor.

The Copies of THE WORLD Printed and Sold on Sunday Last Aggregated **230,220.** The Average Circulation of THE SUNDAY WORLD is Larger than that of any other Newspaper Published on the Western Hemisphere.

The World.

The Copies of THE WORLD Printed and Sold on Sunday Last Aggregated **230,220.** The Average Circulation of THE SUNDAY WORLD is Larger than that of any other Newspaper Published on the Western Hemisphere.

VOL. XXVI., NO. 8,757. NEW YORK, TUESDAY, AUGUST 11, 1885—WITH SUPPLEMENT. PRICE TWO CENTS.

THE SPECTRE IN GRANADA.

A CONDITION MORE HORRIBLE THAN THAT OF NAPLES LAST YEAR.

DEPRESSION IN BRITISH TRADE.

Discussing Its Causes in the House of Lords—Prorogation of Parliament.

MURDERED IN HIS HOME.

A WEALTHY BROOKLYNITE SHOT DOWN BY A HIDDEN FOE.

ONE HUNDRED THOUSAND DOLLARS!

TRIUMPHANT COMPLETION OF THE WORLD'S FUND FOR THE LIBERTY PEDESTAL.

Story of the Greatest Popular Subscription Ever Raised in America—How the Republic Was Saved from Lasting Disgrace—An Event for Patriotic Citizens to Rejoice Over—A Roll of Honor Bearing the Names of 120,000 Generous Patriots—The Flags of France and the American Union Floating in Sisterly Sympathy—Over $3,300 Received Yesterday—The Grand Total Foots Up $102,006.39—A Generous Lady Pays $130 for the Washington Cent.

Statue of Liberty's pedestal on Bedloe's Island

The Statue Rises in New York

Once the pedestal was done, workers put the pieces of the statue together. First, they built the metal framework. Then they attached each piece of copper. Finally, the statue was finished!

Dangerous Work
In the United States, many of the workers who pieced together the statue and built the pedestal were immigrants. They had dangerous jobs. Some hung from ropes high in the air to do their work. Their efforts and sacrifices made it possible to complete the Statue of Liberty.

Words to Know
IMMIGRANT: A person who comes to a country to live there permanently

a guest badge from the statue's dedication ceremony

About a million people celebrated the statue's dedication at a parade in New York City.

a souvenir medal from the ceremony's celebration

On October 28, 1886, a ceremony on Bedloe's Island made it official. U.S. president Grover Cleveland gave a speech. Sadly, Laboulaye died before the statue was finished, but Bartholdi was there. Bartholdi removed the French flag to reveal Lady Liberty's face. The crowd cheered.

Welcoming Immigrants

In 1892, an immigration station opened on Ellis Island. When immigrants arrived in New York, they were taken to this station. Bedloe's Island, with the statue standing tall, was nearby.

For the next 62 years, more than 12 million immigrants from countries all over the world arrived at Ellis Island. They all passed by the Statue of Liberty on their way.

a group of immigrants arriving at Ellis Island

the immigration station on Ellis Island

A boat carrying immigrants passes the statue on its way to Ellis Island in New York Harbor.

Many of the immigrants arriving in New York left difficult lives in their home countries. They wanted a better life in the United States for themselves and their families.

New arrivals came on crowded ships. Some had traveled for weeks. They were exhausted.

Immigrants wait to be processed on Ellis Island.

An immigrant family stands with their belongings on Ellis Island.

As these ships entered the harbor, one of the first things the immigrants on board saw was the statue. Lady Liberty welcomed them to their new home.

A poet named Emma Lazarus worked to help new immigrants in New York. She wrote a poem about the statue and the experience of newcomers to the country.

Over many years, her poem "The New Colossus" became famous. The poem is about welcoming immigrants from other countries. The Statue of Liberty guides them toward a new life in the United States.

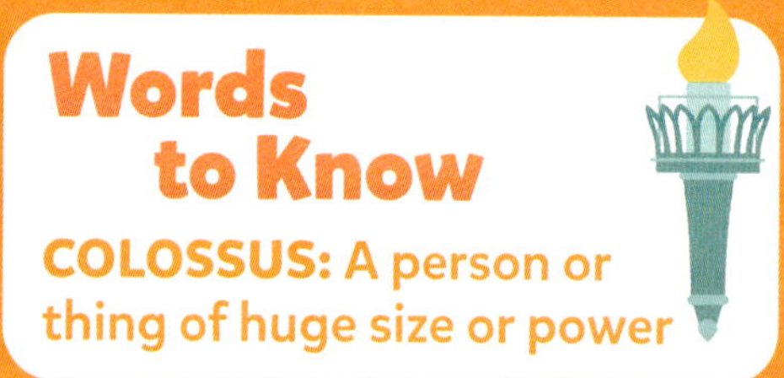

Famous Lines
There is a part of Lazarus's poem that many people know and can say from memory:

"Give me your tired, your poor,
Your huddled masses yearning to breathe free,
The wretched refuse of your teeming shore.
Send these, the homeless, tempest-tost to me,
I lift my lamp beside the golden door!"

Visitors can read this famous poem on a plaque inside the Statue of Liberty's pedestal.

THE NEW COLOSSUS.

NOT LIKE THE BRAZEN GIANT OF GREEK FAME,
WITH CONQUERING LIMBS ASTRIDE FROM LAND TO LAND;
HERE AT OUR SEA-WASHED, SUNSET GATES SHALL STAND
A MIGHTY WOMAN WITH A TORCH, WHOSE FLAME
IS THE IMPRISONED LIGHTNING, AND HER NAME
MOTHER OF EXILES. FROM HER BEACON-HAND
GLOWS WORLD-WIDE WELCOME; HER MILD EYES COMMAND
THE AIR-BRIDGED HARBOR THAT TWIN CITIES FRAME.
"KEEP ANCIENT LANDS, YOUR STORIED POMP!"
CRIES SHE
WITH SILENT LIPS. "GIVE ME YOUR TIRED, YOUR
POOR,
YOUR HUDDLED MASSES YEARNING TO BREATHE FREE,
THE WRETCHED REFUSE OF YOUR TEEMING SHORE.
SEND THESE, THE HOMELESS, TEMPEST-TOST TO ME,
I LIFT MY LAMP BESIDE THE GOLDEN DOOR!"

THIS TABLET, WITH HER SONNET TO THE BARTHOLDI STATUE
OF LIBERTY ENGRAVED UPON IT, IS PLACED UPON THESE WALLS
IN LOVING MEMORY OF
EMMA LAZARUS
BORN IN NEW YORK CITY, JULY 22ND 1849
DIED NOVEMBER 19TH, 1887.

This bronze plaque was presented by philanthropist Georgiana Schuyler in 1903, twenty years after Emma Lazarus wrote her sonnet. Originally displayed on the interior wall of the Statue of Liberty's pedestal, it was placed in this exhibit in July, 1986.

Lots of Lady Liberties

Washington, Kansas

Fairfield, Iowa

Leicester, England

Colorado Springs, Colorado

Salisbury, Missouri

Dallas, Texas

Cadaqués, Spain

Buenos Aires, Argentina

There are sculptures modeled after the Statue of Liberty all over the world. Here's a map of some of them. Can you find a Statue of Liberty sculpture near you?

Restoring the Statue

Over time, parts of the Statue of Liberty broke down. The support skeleton was rusting. The torch had water damage. Holes appeared in the statue's copper.

A large project to restore the statue was finished in time for the 100th anniversary in 1986. Workers replaced iron support bars with steel. A new torch was put in place. In the end, the work took two years and cost almost $70 million.

That's a FACT!

Today, visitors can see the old torch in the Statue of Liberty Museum on Liberty Island.

restorations of the crown in 1938

Closed After Disasters

Over the years, the Statue of Liberty has closed only a few times. After the terrorist attacks on September 11, 2001, the statue closed for safety reasons. It reopened to visitors on August 3, 2004.

The statue also closed after Hurricane Sandy hit in 2012. About eight months of repairs from flood damage were done before the statue reopened.

work to restore the statue for the 100th anniversary

The Statue of Liberty Today

Today, about four million people visit the Statue of Liberty every year. Visitors can go to the top of the pedestal to an observation deck. From there, they can take the stairs to Liberty's crown. Windows in the crown offer spectacular views of New York City, the harbor, and Ellis Island.

Boats carry visitors to and from Liberty Island.

1871
Bartholdi travels to the U.S. to find a site.

1875
Laboulaye and Franco-American Committee approve Bartholdi's statue design.

1875–1880
French committee raises money for statue.

1876
Construction of statue begins in Paris.

inside the Statue of Liberty Museum on Liberty Island

In 2019, the Statue of Liberty Museum opened on Liberty Island. The museum's exhibits tell visitors about the statue's long history.

1877–1885
American committee raises money for pedestal.

1883
Laboulaye dies.

1884
Statue completed in France. Pedestal construction begins in U.S.

1885
Statue taken apart and shipped to U.S.

Over the years, the Statue of Liberty has meant different things to different people.

For some, like Laboulaye, the statue was a symbol of freedom and democracy. To many of the immigrants passing through Ellis Island, she was a symbol of hope for a better life.

March–August 1885
Pulitzer raises money for pedestal.

June 17, 1885
Statue arrives in New York and is placed in storage.

1886
Statue's pedestal is finished.

October 23, 1886
Last copper piece placed on statue.

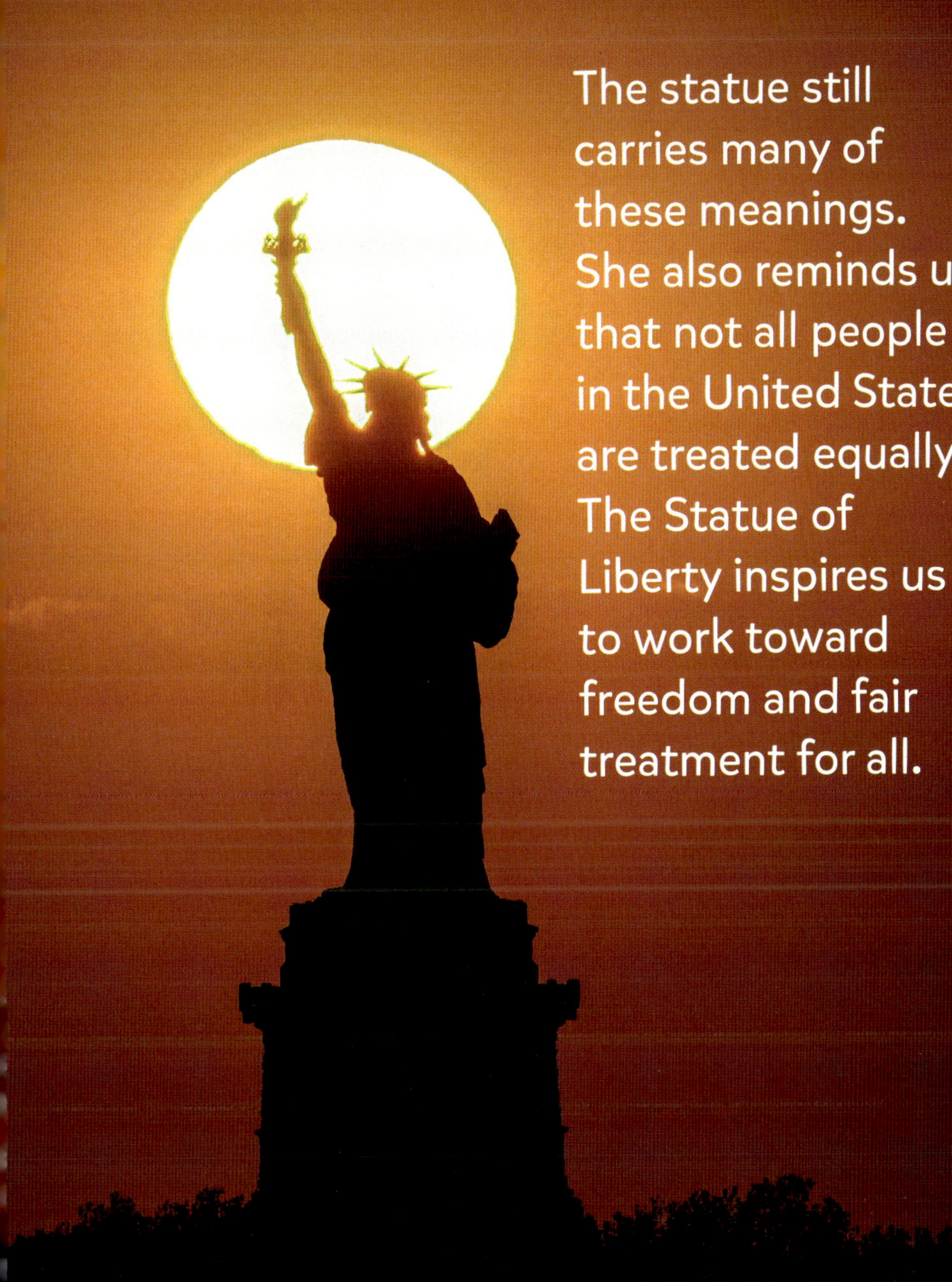

The statue still carries many of these meanings. She also reminds us that not all people in the United States are treated equally. The Statue of Liberty inspires us to work toward freedom and fair treatment for all.

October 28, 1886
Dedication celebration and unveiling.

1956
Bedloe's Island is renamed Liberty Island.

1984–1986
100th anniversary restoration of statue.

Quiz Whiz

1 **Who designed the Statue of Liberty?**

A. George Washington
B. Richard Morris Hunt
C. Frédéric-Auguste Bartholdi
D. Joseph Pulitzer

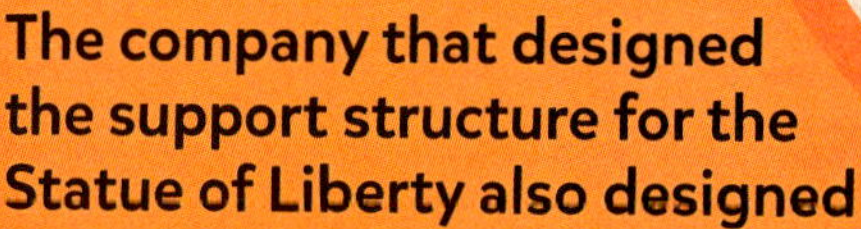

2 **The company that designed the support structure for the Statue of Liberty also designed ____________________.**

A. the Empire State Building
B. the Eiffel Tower
C. the Washington Monument
D. Big Ben

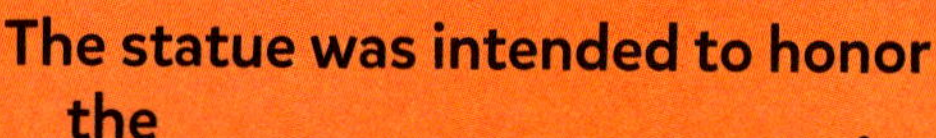

3 **The statue was intended to honor the ____________________.**

A. anniversary of U.S. independence from British rule
B. long friendship between France and the United States
C. end of the enslavement of people in the United States
D. all of the above

4

What year was the statue completed in New York Harbor?

A. 1886
B. 1776
C. 1986
D. 1920

5

How many copper sheets is the statue made of?

A. 12
B. 163
C. 175
D. more than 300

6

About how tall is the statue, including the pedestal?

A. 305 feet (93 m)
B. 273 feet (83 m)
C. 215 feet (65.5 m)
D. 100 feet (30.5 m)

7

Who wrote the famous poem about the statue, "The New Colossus"?

A. Amanda Gorman
B. Emma Lazarus
C. Robert Frost
D. Emily Dickinson

The New Colossus.
Not like the brazen giant of Greek fame,
With conquering limbs astride from land to land;
Here at our sea-washed, sunset gates shall stand
A mighty woman with a torch, whose flame
Is the imprisoned lightning, and her name
Mother of Exiles. From her beacon-hand
Glows world-wide welcome; her mild eyes command
The air-bridged harbor that twin-cities frame.
"Keep, ancient lands, your storied pomp!" cries she
With silent lips. "Give me your tired, your poor,
Your huddled masses yearning to breathe free,
The wretched refuse of your teeming shore,
Send these, the homeless, tempest-tost to me,
I lift my lamp beside the golden door!"

Answers: 1. C, 2. B, 3. D, 4. A, 5. D, 6. A, 7. B

Glossary

Colossus

A person or thing of huge size or power

Declaration of Independence

A document stating that the American colonies were free from British control

Democracy

A system of government where the people have a say in the country's laws and policies

Enlightening

Helping a person understand something better

Enslavement

The act of making someone a slave

Freedom
The right to think, speak, or act as you want

Immigrant
A person who comes to a country to live there permanently

Independence
The state of not being controlled by others

Pedestal
A platform or base that supports a statue

Represent
To stand for something else

Symbol
An object or thing that stands for something else, such as another idea

Index

National Geographic Kids Readers

for curious kids at every reading level!

Pre-reader • Ready to read

Level 1 Co-reader • Starting to read together

Level 1 • Starting to read

Level 2 • Reading independently

Fluent reader

Level 3 books are ideal for kids who are reading on their own with ease and are ready for more challenging vocabulary and varied sentence structures.

Manufactured in the United States of America

rhcbooks.com | @randomhousekids

US $5.99/ $7.99 CAN

ISBN 978-1-4263-7828-7